ROSEMARY RUDDLE'S
RUTLAND RECIPES

LEICESTERSHIRE LIBRARIES AND INFORMATION SERVICE

Printed by Ratnett & Co. Ltd., Knighton Junction Lane,
Welford Road, Leicester.

Acknowledgements

A great many people have helped me to compile these recipes and reminiscences.

First, I would like to thank my mother, Lady Ruddle; Mrs. Margery Brewin for testing and advising on many recipes; Miss Margaret Harper, Head of Library & Information Services for East Leicestershire, for help with the initial research; Mrs. Brenda Tew and Mrs. April Boyse both of whom were kind enough to read the manuscript.

Then I must remember the people, some of them mentioned by name in the text, whom I met through friends, the W.I, local newspapers, or simply accosted in village streets or shops; many of these invited me into their homes, gave their time and knowledge, and often entrusted me with their treasured, old, family, recipe books.

Acknowledgements are also due to the following publishers who kindly allowed me to quote from their publications: *Food and Drink in Britain* by C. Anne Wilson, published by Constable 1973; *Food in England* by Dorothy Hartley, published by Macdonald and Jones 1955; *Good Things in England* by Florence White, published by Jonathan Cape 1932 (now available in paperback by Futura Books); and *Lark Rise to Candleford* by Flora Thompson, published by Oxford University Press 1954; Penguin 1973.

Without the encouragement of Mrs. Elizabeth David I would never have started to collect the recipes; without her practical suggestions and help they would never have turned into a book. My thanks are also due to the County Librarian and his staff, in particular to Mr. David Antill, Librarian, Publications & Public Relations. Finally, thank you to my husband for all his support, and for eating and commenting constructively on the many dishes tested for this book.

Preface

'*Okeham*, that ftands below, in diftance near,
(The Capital both of the Vale and Shire)
Though fmall and humble in her lowly Seat,
Thinks of her Neighbourhood, grows proud
                                    and great . . .
As *Rutland* has been *England's* Garden writ,
So this muft be allow'd th 'Epitome of it.'*

The epitome being referred to by James Wright was the stately home which had recently been erected at Burley on the Hill. Rutland's first County Historian obviously possessed an intense pride in the natural landscape, the old county families, and the architectural monuments—the Churches and Mansion Houses of England's (sometime) smallest county.

This publication attempts to recapture the somewhat less grandiose aspects of the county's history; namely the domestic activities of ordinary country folk. I have tried to record the way people lived, *what they ate* and how they entertained themselves in Rutland in days gone by.

Readers may like to try their hand at some of these recipes, but whether their interest is primarily gastronomic or historical I hope that this book will play its part in keeping alive the memory of our county traditions.

Rosemary Ruddle

*from:

The History and Antiquities of the County of Rutland by James Wright. Originally published 1684-1714, for B. Griffin, London.

Acknowledgements

Preface

CONTENTS

Rutland Shire (Map) *Cartographer: J. Rocque*—1753

Appendix

Clipsham   Plough Boys' Song—
     (Mummers' Play)

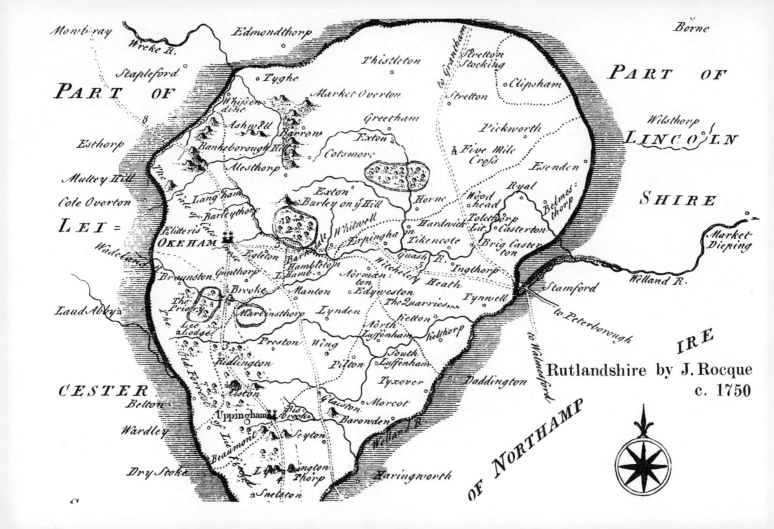

Rutlandshire by J. Rocque
c. 1750

Chapter 1

Keeping the Village Feast

A hundred years ago Feast days meant more to most village people than Christmas. The Feast was the celebration of the village saint's day, and in some places it is still a church festival. In the past it had a way of stretching into a week of festivities during which farm workers and boys were given a holiday. The Sunday of the Feast is described in Flora Thompson's lovely book about her childhood in an isolated Oxfordshire hamlet at the end of the last century:

"Then strangers, as well as friends, came from far and near to throng the houses and the inn and to promenade on the stretch of road which ran through the hamlet. On that day the big ovens were heated and nearly every family managed to have a joint of beef and a Yorkshire Pudding for dinner. The men wore their best suits, complete with collar and tie, and the women brought out their treasured finery and wore it, for, even if no relatives from a distance were expected, someone might be 'popping in', if not to dinner, to tea or supper. Half a crown at least had been saved from the harvest money for spending at the inn, and the jugs and beer-cans went merrily round the Rise.

" 'Arter all, 'tis the Feast', they said; 'an't only comes once a year' and they enjoyed the extra food and drink and the excitement of seeing so many people about, never dreaming that they were celebrating the dedication five hundred years before of the little old church in the mother village which so few of them attended".*

These feasts were common all over Britain and Europe and in some parts of Spain and France are still celebrated. In Rutland it is some years since any village kept its feast in the old style. Village people have regular entertainment now, they have cars and buses to go to local towns, they have proper holidays and can go on package tours. The days are past when a good meal, a few stalls selling trinkets, a hurdie-gurdie perhaps, and dancing on the green to the tunes of a local fiddler, constituted an occasion to look forward to all year. If some of us regret the passing of this pleasant custom, we should remember that it was a hard, monotonous life and be glad that conditions have improved. However, the recipes for feast dishes are still remembered and are often the most interesting of local specialities. I think it is worth while recording them and some of the anecdotes and reminiscences that go with them.

* From *Lark Rise to Candleford* by Flora Thompson, 1973 Penguin.

Cottesmore: The Village

From: Victoria County History of Rutland. Vol II

In Ridlington the baker would devote a day to baking pies, lemon curd tarts and cheesecakes ready for the feast on the first Sunday after July 22nd. On the Sunday, roasts were eaten, usually beef, and these were often cooked as was then the custom, in the baker's oven. The joints, with their accompanying Yorkshire Pudding batter in a jug would be taken on the way to church; the charge was a penny, though it had gone up to twopence before the custom died.

1. Lemon Curd

Well beat two eggs in a basin and add half a pound of sugar and two ounces of butter, the juice of two lemons and their rind. Stand the basin in a saucepan of boiling water, stirring till it thickens. This may be bottled and stored or used to fill pastry cases. Lemon curd can sometimes be bought at the Women's Institute market held each Friday morning in Oakham.

There were roundabouts and coconut shies on Ridlington Green and in the pub yard; in the evening there were dances in a barn—such things as the Cross Hand Polka, Heel and Toe Polka, and Up and Down the Middle were danced.

Traditionally on Feast Monday a cricket match took place between Wing and Ridlington. It started at eleven o'clock and ended at seven o'clock and an old couple known as Adam and Eve would fiddle the players in and out. One person told me that a pigeon was sent to Wing with the result. This match was held annually for at least fifty years.

In Langham many people remember when not only farm workers were on holiday but the brewery closed for the week. Like so many of the villages in the diocese of Peterborough, Langham's Feast is St. Peter's, the first Sunday after June 29th. Langham people ate roast duck, their first garden peas and new potatoes, followed by curd tarts.

There would be a fair on what is now Fairfields Close, with hurdy-gurdies and a fiddler from the market town of Oakham. Cricket matches went on all week; the teams would lunch at the Noel Arms, sometimes so heartily that replacements were necessary for the afternoon. In the evenings people often kept open house with a ham to cut (sometimes baked, sometimes cooked in beer or cider) and *Feast Cakes* to eat.

2. Langham Feast Cake

These are the traditional ingredients from a recipe given to me by Miss Ellingworth of Oakham, well known for her local knowledge:

2 lbs flour	1 lb lard
½ lb brown sugar	1 nutmeg
1 lb currants	2 ozs lemon peel

3 ozs lemon kailey (*this is like sherbet, but is no longer obtainable: it acted as a raising agent*).

These were mixed well with water and baked in a slow oven. As Miss Ellingworth said, this was "a cake for times when families were large and money short".

Langham cricket team's regular opponent on the Monday of Feast week was Whissendine. Their Feast falls on the Sunday following July 13th and is remembered as a time when people working away from home were reunited with their families. A band played for the church service and afterwards on the Green. During the week there were garden parties on the vicarage lawn when a string band, composed mainly of the parish maiden ladies' played. In the evenings there were dances, entrance threepence; Wednesday was devoted to Country Dances which were strictly supervised by older ladies who knew the figures. I have been unable to find any dishes peculiar to Whissendine, but there is one curious custom concerning the field where, during the Feast, the fair was held. The Banks, as it is named, belongs to the Parish Council. Each year an auction is held at which a pin is stuck in a candle, the candle lit, and the last person to bid before the pin falls rents the field for that price for a year. (In 1896 it fetched £4 12s. 6d.—recently it went for fifteen pounds).

Cottesmore celebrated its Feast on July 25th, St. James's day, as its own Saint's day (St. Nicholas) is in December. Like Langham, this village was famous for *curd tarts, or cheesecakes*, at Feast time. There is some confusion here—the two names are interchangeable now, it seems.

Anne C. Wilson in *Food and Drink in Britain* says: "Curds were still incorporated in certain cooked dishes which had survived from medieval times. The spiced cheese tarts of that period were continued in tarts of curds which were still known as cheesecakes in the seventeenth century as they are today. Fresh curds formed the basis of the filling, supported by eggs, spices and sometimes currants. By the middle of the century some cheesecake recipes contained neither cheese nor curds, but instead a rich custard mixture of eggs, butter, flour and unrenneted cream, duly sweetened and spiced.

A further development a few decades later was the *lemon cheesecake*. Its filling consisted of pounded lemon peel, egg yolks, sugar and butter; in fact it was what we now call "*Lemon-cheese or Lemon-curd*".

Although it has not been kept since the 1930's Mrs. Hollis told me that older people in Cottesmore remember when the main street was blocked by people, horses and traps; all who could get to a local Feast did so. Hence the making of hundreds of curd tarts in every household ready for anyone calling in. One family has some enormous meat dishes which they say were piled high with the tarts; another family with a similar recipe remembers the tarts in a net slung from the ceiling.

Similar traditions surround the *Yorkshire Wilfra Tarts* baked to celebrate the Feast of the patron saint of Ripon Cathedral, I believe, and of Melton Mowbray in neighbouring Leicestershire it was said (in *Good Things in England*, Edited by Florence White):

"At the Whitsuntide Feast enough cheesecakes are made and eaten to pave the whole town". Indeed many English counties have a variation of this most ancient dish. The American writer M. F. K. Fisher (in *Bold Knife and Fork*), talking about its origins, says: "It moved with all the benign as well as corrupt attributes of culture from the East and Near East into Greece and Rome, and in the almost intolerably lengthy banquet described by Athenaeus in the second century AD and called *The Deipnosophists*, many pages are devoted to it".

More prosaically, here is an excellent recipe given by Mrs. Betty Hollis of Cottesmore, as made, she says, by her grandmother-in-law:

3. Lemon Cheesecake

½ lb curd*	1 *tablespoon brandy*
¼ lb butter	2 *ozs currants*
¼ lb castor sugar	1 *oz lemon peel*
3 eggs—leaving out one white	*Nutmeg*

Cream butter and sugar, add the beaten eggs and other ingredients. Break the curd with a fork and add. Put into shortcrust lined tart tins and bake for about 40 minutes in a preheated oven (350°, gas 3-4) until slightly brown.

* *some Supermarkets sell curd cheese (not to be confused with cottage cheese), but probably nearer to the real thing is the ricotta cheese sold in many Italian shops and delicatessens.*

These quantities fill two six-inch tins.

Sometimes a spot of whisky was added instead of brandy; either is a great improvement. Miss Ellingworth says about the curds themselves: "Langham and Whissendine cheesecakes are not the same these days as farmers' wives made the curds from their own milk".

Incidentally, if anyone has access to fresh milk (milk warm from the cow is best) half a gallon makes enough curd to make the above recipe.

This is an interesting and rather more substantial version containing hard-boiled eggs:

4. Lemon Cheesecake with hard-boiled eggs

¼ lb butter	3 oz sugar
¼ lb currants	1 small beaten egg
1½ tablespoons brandy	lemon peel
2 hard-boiled eggs	

Chop the hard-boiled eggs and mix them with the creamed butter and sugar, adding the peel, currants, brandy and lastly the beaten egg. This amount will fill two eight inch pastry cases. Bake at about 400° (gas 5) for half an hour.

Mrs. Barbara Palmer who gave me the recipe says: "I cannot guarantee its origin, but it was given to my mother by her very old friend and could be pre-First World War". I can only describe it as rather like mince pies with a lot of brandy butter.

Braunston, famous for its cheeses (see chapter 4) kept their Feast on the first Sunday after October 10th—one of the latest in the county. The two pubs used to take turns to "serve the feast", usually roast beef and plum pudding apparently, although at least in one home they ate roast duck (like Langham) and another used to make this *Barm Spice Cake* (in extremely large quantities, like so many of these recipes).

5. Barm Spice Cake

2 lbs plain flour	¾ lb lard
1¼ lbs sugar	1 oz yeast
3 eggs	¼ lb butter
1 lb currants	½ lb raisins
1 teaspoon Bicarbonate of Soda	a little salt
nutmeg or mixed spice	

Rub butter and lard into flour. Add fruit and sugar. Put yeast in a basin with a little tepid water, dissolve the Bicarbonate of Soda in a little milk, and add them both to the beaten eggs. Mix liquid into dry ingredients to powdered cake. Let it stand all night, put in tins and bake at 325° (gas 3-4) for 2½ hours. This amount filled a six inch and an eight inch tin, and it was thought to make a good lunch cake.

Mrs. Hennegan from the Post Office at Braunston, who gave me this recipe remarks that in spite of the yeast it does not rise overnight.

Miss Meadowes, whose family have farmed in the village for many years, remembered a decorated pig's head, an orange in its mouth, on display in the butcher's window preceding the Feast, and then carried round the village, no doubt amid appreciation both artistic and gastronomic. But, as a small girl, she liked best the many different-coloured blancmanges made at Feast time.

In North Luffenham—their saint is John the Baptist—on June 24th, they have several excellent Feast dishes: a *rabbit pie*, and an *egg and bacon pie*, both eaten cold, and a *lardie cake* eaten hot straight from the oven.

6. Rabbit Pie

Rabbit Pie is often eaten hot, stewing beef or ham being added. *Here, however, the rabbit joints are first stewed in water with an onion and a bunch of fresh herbs; this water is used to make a stock for the pie, so include a pig's trotter or two so that it will set to a jelly later. The stock will have to be simmered for some hours after the joints are cooked. Fill the deep pie dish with the boned rabbit, plenty of hard-boiled eggs cut in quarters, some chopped parsley and any other fresh herbs you like: pour in the strained stock before covering with a short crust which can be decorated with leaves or other patterns. It is important to make a hole with a funnel in the centre or the pastry will go soggy as it cools. Bake in a medium hot oven until the pastry is a nice brown. Leave overnight for the jelly to set.*

This would normally be served with home-made pickles, and it is as well to remember that if you accompany it with hot vegetables of any kind they will probably melt the aspic, made as it is without commercial gelatine.

Egg and Bacon Pie is, of course, another ancient dish, made all over the country. In some parts it is an open tart, in others covered; in some counties the eggs are beaten with milk, in others left whole, or lightly pricked. In Shropshire they are careful to place each egg on a piece of bacon, or ham; in Yorkshire it is sometimes made in a dripping tin and cut into squares when cold. In Buckinghamshire they make a saucer pie (the pastry being cut to line a saucer in which the pie is baked) which is convenient for lunch in the fields.

Today this homely dish is extremely fashionable in London "country" restaurants and food stores under the name of *Quiche Lorraine*.

In North Luffenham they make a *"top and bottom" pie. That is to say, you line an old-fashioned shallow pie plate with short crust, place diced bacon on the bottom, break the eggs on top, add salt and pepper, and cover with pastry.* It can be eaten hot, but in these parts it is more usually consumed cold.

7. Lardie Cakes

Lardie Cakes are sometimes called *Lard or Flead Cakes;* in some places they are made with a piece of bread dough left over from the main baking, and they sometimes contain spice such as nutmeg, cinnamon or allspice. In this recipe self-raising flour is used:

10 *oz self-raising flour*	5 *oz pure pork lard*
6 *oz currants*	4 *oz caster sugar*
1 *egg well beaten*	1 *cup of milk*
a pinch of salt	

Rub the fat into the flour with the salt. Add sugar, egg and milk. Beat well and add fruit last. Bake in a shallow tin, a Yorkshire Pudding tin for example, at 375° (gas 4-5) for an hour. Score the dough across so that it will break easily when cooked. Eat while hot, with or without butter.

Other Feastday memories and impressions were sketchy. In Preston, Teigh (Tit-tattling Teigh they call it), Ketton, Market Overton, Greetham (Grievous Greetham), whose band was so much in demand at other villages' feasts, Harringworth and others I could find no one who remembered any special dishes.

The writer Marcel Boulestin, an anglophile if ever a Frenchman was, had the same problem. In *A Second Helping* (published in 1925) he said: "Up till now I had not been able to discover in England any autochthonous dishes (excepting of course, the classical things like steak and kidney pie, lamb and mint sauce, and various steamed puddings) but now I have tasted some which are delicious and no doubt there are more, somewhere in Yorkshire maybe; though when you ask an Englishman about these honest local dishes he is curiously reticent about, or ignorant of them".

In Glaston someone remembered a band and dancing in the street; a man would come out from Stamford with his horse and trap and set out trays of pretty sweets—a good handful could be bought for a halfpenny and a large ice cream cornet for one penny.

In Exton a dinner took place in the barn behind the Fox and Hounds, roundabouts and swings were set up in the school yard; they tried "to dig their first potatoes for Feast Sunday".

At the tiny hamlet of Burley there were concerts in the blacksmith's shop; Grandma Lane (a name that has been connected with this village for so long) would "cook a ham and put a frill on it".

The church service is all that remains of the habit of keeping the feast in most villages, although in some they gather afterwards for refreshments. In Ayston, for example, they meet in an old and very beautiful barn belonging to Mr. Robinson. At the beginning of this century though, this village had a band from Kettering, as well as the locally famous fiddlers, Adam and Eve Smith, to celebrate their feast. Fairy lights were strung across the street (and thought to be a marvellous innovation) and they danced on the lawn in front of the Rector's farmhouse. There were fireworks too, and a cricket match.

Chapter 2

Lesser Feasts

In a life which followed a strict monotonous routine, when holidays as we know them now did not exist, Feast days and other small festivals were important.

Valentine's Day was marked, in Uppingham, by the giving of gingerbreads to lovers and, in Market Overton, "maids" were given a Valentine Day bun, known as a *Rutland Plum Shuttle*.

8. Plum Shuttles

The original *Plum Shuttles* are made in the following way, the recipe for which was given to me by Miss Ellingworth:

1½ lbs plain flour	4 oz butter
4 oz castor sugar	4 oz clean currants
2 oz chopped peel	1 oz yeast
½ pint milk and ½ pint water to mix	

Warm a large mixing bowl, sift the flour into it. Rub in the fat until the mixture resembles breadcrumbs. Sprinkle in sugar, reserving a teaspoonful, add currants and peel. Mix well.

Crumble yeast with teaspoonful of sugar and mix until it liquefies. Add to flour and stir in milk and water, adding more water if necessary (or indeed more flour if necessary) to make a soft dough. Leave for about 30 minutes to prove. Turn the dough on a lightly floured board and knead until smooth. Pull into pieces and shape into small ovals, about the size of a sausage with pointed ends (in fact, the shape of a weaver's shuttle). Arrange the shuttles on a warm baking sheet and leave in a warm place for 20 minutes to prove.

Bake in the centre of a pre-heated oven 425° (gas 7) for 15 to 20 minutes.

These are sometimes made with caraway seeds as well as currants, but originally this was not so. They are quite big and filling and constituted a meal on their own. Nowadays they would find a place perhaps at tea time, made slightly smaller and served hot if possible with butter—they are excellent eaten like this.

These same buns were given, with a glass of ale and a shilling, to farm workers on **Plough Monday,** the first Monday after Twelfth Night. Plough Monday was "the beginning of the agricultural season and the beginning of ploughing before it became common to do any winter sowing". (J. Oliver in *Milk, Cheese and Butter*, published in 1894.)

The boys from different farms would get together to perform a traditional one-act play in some villages; they wore costumes and, accompanied by music, went round all the houses. Clipsham was well-known for this and the full script given to me by Mrs. Wilson of Clipsham is reproduced in the Appendix.

On this occasion (Plough Monday) the *Plum Shuttles* were called *Stattes Buns*. Stattes, or sometimes statices, means a hiring. **The Hiring Fair** was also known as the Statute Fair from which stattes and statices must derive. In some places the Hiring was an elaborate affair. Mr. Capendale has given me a very good account of the Ketton Hirings that took place each Martinmas. The last was held on November 16th, 1901.

"Men and women offering themselves for employment assembled in front of the Midland Hotel. Each wore a token in his buttonhole to indicate his calling: a carter sported a piece of whipcord, a shepherd a wisp of wool, while a plait of straw betokened a cowman. Farmers and their wives from a wide area mingled with the would-be employees discussing details of interest, for both were bound by law to keep their side of any agreement.

When a bargain had been reached the farmer handed over a coin, usually a shilling, and the person then replaced his token with a piece of ribbon to show that he was now hired.

The business of the morning over, the rest of the day was spent in jollification. At the last Ketton Statice there were travelling showmen with their coconut shies, skittles, donkey rides, and Station Lane was lined with stalls heaped with white gingerbread rock, cobnuts, trinkets and ornaments".

Club Feasts—Before the National Health Service there were many clubs such as this. My source is Mr. Capendale again:

"A club known as the 'Ketton Amicable Friendly Club' functioned from about 1870 or 1880, and its main objects were to help the working people of the village with Sick Pay and to provide the services of a Doctor free of charge. Members paid four shilling per quarter and received Sick Pay at the rate of eight shillings per week. The Doctor's services were contracted by the Club at a cost of four shillings per member per year. Death Benefits of six pounds and three pounds respectively were paid for member and wife.

The Club held an Annual Feast on the First Thursday in June, when members assembled at the Northwick Hall in the morning. On handing over a metal check each member received at the hands of the Club Stewards a pint of ale and bread and cheese. The assembly then paraded to church, headed by a band, generally the village band but on occasion one from Oakham. Following a short service, a dinner was held back at the Northwick Hall when the fare included roast beef, plum pudding and plenty of ale, a barrel being set up in the room for the occasion.

The annual meeting of the Club succeeded the dinner.

During the evening of the Annual Dinner the members would tour the village with the band, calling at the various public houses and more important mansions where their jugs of ale were replenished, returning eventually to the Northwick Hall where a dance concluded the festivities. Invariably present were the Vicar and the Doctor, and the fare was provided by the village tradesmen".

The **weekly markets** in Uppingham were a time for friends to meet as well as do business. The cattle and sheep were in the main market place, the pigs in the yard of the Rose and Crown, one of the sixteen pubs in the town at the time. Stray beasts were herded into a pinfold on the outskirts of the town till claimed (or until their owners came out of the pubs).

Uppingham had, and indeed still has, a **fair** each March. In the old days the fairground equipment came by train and was fetched from the station by traction engines (which, incidentally, later saw service in France during the First World War). There were merry-go-rounds, accompanied by organ music, stalls with sugar candy on a string and other sweets, all lit by charcoal burners until these went out, as they invariably did, and were replaced by paraffin flares which cast strange shadows.

But the high spots of Uppingham's year were really the **Flower Show** and **Sports Thursday** in the Summer. The entrance to the latter was a shilling and if your ticket had a lucky number you might win a new bicycle. Once in you could watch running and bicycle races, and horse trotting. After the Flower Show there were bands and dancing, albeit on the rough grass—if you fell over a molehill, taking your partner down with you, well, it was Feast Week and, as one now elderly gentleman said: "there was no malice".

May Day was celebrated (by children dancing round the maypole and crowning the May Queen), as was **Harvest Festival** in most villages.

Harvest Suppers continued in many villages even during the last war. Farmers, of course, had an extra allowance of cheese, fats for cooking, sugar and tea. In Rutland their extra workers were often airmen stationed locally. Farmers now rely more on machines than on extra labourers, so the pleasant custom of Harvest Suppers seems to have died.

The Supper would usually consist of rabbit pies, home-cured ham, sometimes a cauliflower cheese, apple pies, Stilton, a barrel of beer (there would often be a barrel under the hedge too, during the harvest) and home-made wines.

Sunday Night Suppers—Gastronomically speaking, farmers and their families were certainly the best off in the county for many years. A description of childhood eating by Mrs. Waller of Lyndon who was brought up in Manton, conjured pictures of wonderful country flavours and well-stocked larders. Sunday night supper, she said, was a ritual. People would come to church from other villages (this seems to be a sort of social exchange that went on all round the county), pop in and stay for high supper. This might consist of an ample joint of cold beef and horseradish, always an apple pie, and trifles (and it is obvious that the trifles were made with home-made jams and thick yellow cream from the farm). Thus Sunday nights were themselves special occasions.

By contrast to this plenty, Miss Ellingworth of Oakham told me about the **annual school tea party** when she was headmistress at Edith Weston in the 1920's:

"Someone gave us a pound of butter, someone a pot of jam; the baker made us a fruit cake and a seedy cake—and they thought they had a feast".

Other holidays were few: **Christmas,** of course, with all its traditional trappings for those who could afford it. In Nurse Goodwin's account of life in Ayston at the turn of the century she says: "At Christmas time each family in the village received half a ton of coal and a piece of beef" from the family at the Hall. Some villages were luckier than others in such customs; Ayston had a very small population, most of whom worked at the Hall.

Good Friday was a holiday then and generally used by people with allotments to sow their corn, and *Simnel cakes* and *gingerbread boys* were made and eaten on **Easter Day**.

Chapter 3

The Country Cook

The Romans were probably the first Rutland inhabitants to afford the luxury of gastronomy (and the last for some time). At Market Overton they were very fond of oysters. I quote from a pamphlet entitled *Roman Rutland* (published 1863): "In one hole quantities of oyster shells were found. According to Pliny the British oyster was deservedly famous amongst the Romans and even as early as the reign of Vespasian thought worthy to be carried into Italy".

Until the seventeenth century little of culinary interest appears in the local history books. Then, however, at Burley on the Hill a celebrated "great cold pie" from which emerged a dwarf, was served up for the entertainment of King Charles and his newly-wedded Queen. (The dwarf, Jeffrey Hudson, was later given to the Queen by her host, the Duke of Buckingham, taken to court and subsequently became famous. He was born in Oakham in 1619 and from the age of seven or eight, when he was only eighteen inches high, had been retained in service at Burley.) Although a great success, the dish did not become a local speciality.

Later in the same King's reign a "scarcity of corn in Rutland 1630-31" is referred to in State papers: ". . . there is scarce corn enough in this countye to sustain theire families and seede theire land". It was so bad that the government intervened and "refrayned the Maulsters from excessive makinge of Mault, and have suppressed twenty Alehouses. . ."

James Wright published his famous history of Rutland in 1684. (The History and Antiquities of the County of Rutland. In 1973 a limited edition was reprinted with several additions bringing it up to date.) One can only assume that he was neither greedy nor ever starving for he makes no mention of the people's diet. For many hundreds of years working people must have been more concerned with survival than gastronomy.

The following is the Bill of Fare of Ketton House of Industry (a very dignified name for the work or poor house) and is dated February 1st, 1802, Empingham. I am grateful, once again, to Mr. Capendale for making this available to me. It is probably a fair indication of what the poor were eating at the time.

SUNDAY

For Breakfast	Broth and Bread
Dinner	Broth, Meat and Bread, and Beer
Supper	Bread and cheese, or butter, and Beer

MONDAY	Broth and Bread
	Bread and cheese, or butter, and Beer
	Bread and cheese, or butter, and Beer
TUESDAY	Milk Porridge or Onion Porridge
	Broth and Meat, bread, and Beer
	Bread and cheese, or butter, and Beer
WEDNESDAY	Broth and Bread
	Rice pudding and Beer
	Bread and cheese, or butter, and Beer
THURSDAY	Milk Porridge or Onion Porridge
	Broth and Meat and Bread and Beer
	Bread and cheese, or butter, and Beer
FRIDAY	Broth and Bread
	Suet Pudding and Beer
	Bread and cheese, or butter, and Beer
SATURDAY	Milk Porridge or Onion Porridge
	Ox head and Bread and Beer
	Bread and cheese, or butter, and Beer

Hours

Summer for breakfast 8 o'clock
Winter   ,,   ,,   9 o'clock
Dinner at 1 o'clock the year round
Supper at 7 o'clock

A monotonous diet by any standards but obviously thought by the authorities to be more than adequate for they add: "If any person is found selling Bread, Meat, Cheese, Butter or clothing out of the said House, he shall come before the Committee". The daily beverage was beer from the brewery at Ketton, being at that time much cheaper than either tea or coffee, both considered luxuries.

An article on *Sixty Years of Leicestershire Farming* (in the old Leicestershire and Rutland Magazine) describes how in the 1880's "some old men still wore the smock with a top hat. It was surprising how long a top hat, once perhaps the property of the rector or the magistrate, lasted a farm worker. The smock was worn for two years, the first year for best and the second for work; and thrifty folk kept it by them one year more to use when there was a specially dirty job, such as dung-carting or pond cleaning".

In Ayston at this time, according to Nurse Goodwin who was brought up there: "the men had their cottages free but were not allowed to keep pigs or poultry, their weekly wages on the farm were sixteen shillings, the gamekeepers eighteen shillings, only the head gardener had twenty shillings. But milk from the Hall (skimmed by a strainer) could be had for the fetching at 7.30 each morning, and dripping could be bought at three-pence per pound".

Other farm workers might have had to rent their cottages (two shillings and sixpence was probably the highest rent paid and it was often less) and pay for their milk (threepence a pint and one penny a quart for separated milk—poor families would get a "pint of new and a quart of old") but they might have a pig in the sty and some hens. Most had plenty of vegetables in the garden or allotment.

Looking through family recipe books (often written in beautiful flowing hands but with worn, well-thumbed covers having passed from mother to daughter to grand-daughter) it seems as if the populace lived on boiled and steamed puddings. In fact, the poorer the family the more nearly this was so. If the pudding (it could be savoury or sweet) did not comprise the whole meal, it often preceded the meat to take the edge off appetites. There were, in consequence, many over-fat, but under-nourished, children at this time. There were Marmalade Puddings, Golden Puddings, Bachelors Puddings, Lemon Puddings, Half Pay Puddings, Fig Puddings, Ginger Puddings, Brown Bread Puddings, Canterbury Puddings, Manchester Puddings, Military Puddings, Honey Comb Puddings, Coconut Puddings, Chocolate Puddings, Snow Puddings, Betsy Puddings, Llandudno Puddings, Railway Puddings, Two and Two Puddings, Five Minute Puddings, Buxton Puddings, Cheese Puddings, Carrot Puddings, Pearl Barley Puddings, Rice Puddings and Plum Puddings. Most of these, and countless others, appear in a great many recipe books. Plum Pudding even turns up in a little French book entitled *Les Secrets de la Bonne Table* by B. Renaudet, published in 1931, and the author was given the recipe for this "gateau national d'Angleterre" by a Mrs. Allingham "de Turtle-Cottage, pres d' Oakham dans le Rutland".

Mrs. C. F. Leyel wrote a book devoted to puddings (*Puddings Baked, Boiled, Fried, Steamed, Iced*). In the preface she explains: ". . . puddings as we know them in England and Scotland, made of a mixture of farinaceous foods, with or without animal or vegetable ingredients, seem to be the invention of the Northern races, probably because the colder climates in which they live demand foods with more heating properties". These days most people have found other ways of keeping warm.

One of the more interesting of the steamed or boiled suet puddings is this:

9. Carrot Pudding

$\frac{1}{4}$ *lb grated carrot* $\frac{1}{4}$ *lb breadcrumbs*
$\frac{1}{4}$ *lb suet* $\frac{1}{4}$ *lb flour*
$\frac{1}{4}$ *lb currants*   1 *large tablespoon treacle*
$\frac{3}{4}$ *of the rind of lemon, grated*

Mix well together with milk. Boil in a mould for $1\frac{1}{2}$ *hours.*

15

This may sound strange but carrots are sweet and were commonly used in sweet dishes in the past; it is surprisingly good.

Incidentally, Mrs. Leyel says if you want to "prevent the taste of boiled washing which is sometimes noticeable in a pudding of this kind" you must make a hole to allow the steam to escape as soon as the pudding is cooked. A point worth noting.

This is a homely dish:

10. Baked Cheese Pudding

1 oz butter	½ pint of milk
¼ lb breadcrumbs	2 ozs grated cheese
1 egg	mustard, salt, pepper

Melt the butter in the milk, mix the breadcrumbs, grated cheese, dry mustard, salt and pepper. Pour the milk over this, adding yolk of egg. Whip the white to a stiff froth, stir in lightly. Pour mixture into a well-greased pie dish. Bake 10-15 minutes. A less substantial pudding is made by using two eggs and leaving out the breadcrumbs, then it is a cheese custard.

With obvious pleasure many people have recalled the food they ate in childhood. One lady told me she had never had a rice pudding as creamy as the ones her grandmother used to make (from skim milk and with currants mixed with the rice in a big baking tin) until she stumbled on the trick of sprinkling suet on top of the pudding. Sometimes rice was baked in water and eaten with syrup. Some short sharp instructions for making a Pearl Barley Pudding: (½ teacup of PB to 1 pint of milk, put to soak for an hour then bake in a slow oven for two hours) end firmly "Be sure and cover it over with a *tin* dish"; and the family cook books are full of such hints and instructions.

A couple from Ketton remembered bag puddings (bag and string always washed and ready for use hanging by the stove) and dumplings boiled in water and eaten either with gravy or syrup, and also richer dishes like hams in barleymeal paste, stuffed chine ("two bucketfuls of parsley you need"), cold bony pie, hot spare rib roast in a tin and eaten with apple sauce, pig's face ("pig's were bigger then . . ."), boiled hocks, rabbits, pigeons, rook pie and lambs' tails pie.

The *Stuffed Chine*, a Lincolnshire dish really, was described to me like this by Mrs. Smith of Hambledon: "It was a tradition that it was served in farm houses (together with rook pie) during May Week, i.e., the first week in May when the farm house servants were on holiday. Unmarried farm workers used to have this week's holiday too, when they attended May Fair and changed jobs, shepherds wearing a tuft of wool in their caps, waggoners two or three ears of corn, etc. Stuffed chine was also served at christenings (each of my four children were christened traditionally, though this didn't happen annually as it used to in Victorian times!)

"The joint was salted and about ten to fourteen pounds in weight and was cut from either side of the backbone leaving about five or six inches of flesh each side; this was scored with a sharp knife at $\frac{1}{4}$ inch intervals leaving the rind uncut and then stuffed with fresh parsley, and sometimes with the addition of lettuce leaves and blackcurrant leaves. It was then steamed in a fish kettle or covered in barley meal paste and baked in the oven. Always eaten cold.

"It can be bought in some Lincolnshire shops although it is joints of bacon and not the chine, and I now stuff pieces of bacon myself sometimes—it's scrumptious!"

Another farmer's wife insisted "You loosen the rind but must NOT cut right through. Take marjoram, onion tops, lettuce and a lot of parsley and chop them finely, using a wooden bowl and chopper. Stuff these into the gaps (any surplus can be wrapped in greaseproof paper), wrap the whole thing in cloths carefully and simmer slowly for hours. Eaten cold this is very rich and good".

These are the sort of recipes that are the despair of inexperienced cooks. But for all their lack of accurate information (how much marjoram, what does a lot of parsley mean, how long should it cook?) it sounds a simple and pleasant procedure, the sort of thing handed down by a daughter watching her mother, never written down. If such a thing is jotted down vital steps are often omitted, things the writer would do automatically if she were making the dish.

If, throughout your childhood a stuffed chine was prepared once a week you would know without hesitation how much parsley was needed, indeed you would probably have been sent out to pick it.

This is an age-old problem. Sir Kenelm Digby, for example (in *The Closet of the Emminently Learned Sir Kenelm Digby Knight Opened, Published with his son's Consent* 1669) attempts to clarify some terms. "The handfuls of Herbs are natural large handfuls (as much as you can take up in your hand) not Apothecaries handfuls, which are much less. If a pottle* do not make it work enough to your mind, you may put in a little more. Discretion and experience must regulate that". No doubt those with discretion but no experience can substitute common sense. And those without common sense, well, they just have to learn from their mistakes, I suppose. Incidentally, the Digby family came from Rutland. Sir Kenelm's father, also Kenelm, and mother

(*pottle=a half gallon measure).

Anne, are buried in the church at Stoke Dry where they lived. This Kenelm was Sheriff of Rutland and also MP from the first year of King Edward's reign to the fourteenth of Queen Elizabeth's. Sir Kenelm followed his lead in public service, as well as keeping the marvellous culinary notes which became a classic cookery book, and was published after his death.

Not many people nowadays would fancy a *Rook Pie:* they have gone out of favour partly because only the legs and breasts are used, so many birds must be skinned to produce enough meat, and partly I suspect on account of the unappetisingly sinister look of the birds. Miss Lane lives in a house on the Green at Burley formerly a pub called the Finch's Arms—it still looks rather like a cosy bar parlour, with many copper and brass pans hanging from the ceiling, settles by the hearth and when I went there, there was a noisy piglet being raised by hand. "The old squire used to love a good rook pie" she told me. The legs and breasts are stewed first, then put in the pie dish with hard-boiled eggs, covered with short crust and baked. It is eaten cold, like a chicken pie, and usually accompanied by mustard.

Lambs' Tails Pie is also out of fashion, for much the same reason. You have to scald the tails, remove the wool, joint and stew them with root vegetables, and sometimes barley, before the pie is baked.

Mrs. Bass, a lady now in her 70's, from a Rutland family, remembers happily her mother's and grandmother's cooking for nine children. "Brisket of beef was our favourite, or thick rib, with lovely Yorkshire pudding. Eggs were pickled for the winter and sold at the farmhouse door for one penny each. My granny used to buy us lovely dripping with lovely brown jelly for fourpence per pound. Half a beast cheek cost one shilling and was made into brawn to eat with toast; sheep's head, liver and heart was one shilling or one shilling and sixpence. Stuffed breast of mutton—this dinner cost one shilling and sixpence with vegetables out of the garden—was delicious hot and a delicacy cold. Oh what happy days!"

They may have been happy days for children, but the conditions in which their mothers cooked were not easy. In particular, as Miss Lawrence (Preston) told me, in summer it was too warm to use the kitchen range. "Until the advent of electricity most farmhouses had an open hearth fire and used them in the summer months (instead of the big range), burning wood and sticks off the farm, with a large iron pot hanging over it, in which the water supply was heated, for general use; also kettles hanging too, for making drinks, tea, etc. When electricity came, we gladly set up an electric stove for cooking and also a boiler for hot water".

For many hundreds of years rabbits were plentiful and

18

though the penalties for poaching were dreadful (it seems extraordinary that landlords didn't allow the poor to catch rabbits which, after all, were usually considered to be pests) many impoverished families surreptitiously put a rabbit in the pot under the root vegetables. In Nurse Goodwin's account of life under the fairly benign rule of Sir Arthur Fludyes of Ayston, who inherited his title in 1896, she says: "There were plenty of pheasants, partridges, rabbits and hares in Wardley Woods. The woods at this time were beautifully kept, the ridings always smooth and mossy and the banks with bluebells, primroses, violets and anemones made a lovely picture in the spring. A gamekeeper looked after the woods and shooting parties from the Hall were a regular event".

Beaters were needed here and on other estates. The going rate at this time for a day's beating was about eightpence and two rabbits.

11.   Rabbit Broth

1 *rabbit*	1 *onion*
½ *lb beefsteak*	½ *a turnip*
3 *quarts of water*	*a bayleaf*
a bunch of parsley	*salt and 8 black peppercorns*

Wash the rabbit well and joint it. Put it with the beef-steak, cut into small pieces, into a pan with the water.

Bring slowly to the boil and add the salt and peppercorns just before it boils. Skim carefully. Add the vegetables and herbs. Simmer for 3½ hours. Strain and put into a cool place to get cold before skimming off the fat. For serving add either a little chopped parsley or about one ounce of boiled rice.

This is an elegant consommé rather than a robust broth; it has a beautiful pale clear colour and delicate flavour. Not usually wanting such copious amounts of broth I halve the quantities, using only the legs of the rabbit.

There is no reason why you shouldn't use the stewed joints, after you have strained the liquid, for the following recipe:

12.   Potted Rabbit

Mrs. Castle of Exton told me her mother used to make many potted meats and this was one of them. It's very important to get the seasoning right and Mrs. Castle says the children used to love "tasting nights" and found plenty of excuses to keep trying things.

Unless you are using rabbit joints from the previous recipe, stew the joints (I usually use the legs rather than the back, but you can of course use both) in some water with an onion, carrot, and herbs until the flesh comes away from the bones easily. *Strain and bone. Chop the meat finely. Add the salt, black pepper and nutmeg (this is where the tasting comes in). Press into a pot and cover with melted butter.*

13. Exton Rabbit Savoury

This is taken from *Rutland Recipes* by Janet L. Rankin, a series which appeared from time to time in the *Old Leicestershire and Rutland Magazine*, in this case in the September issue, 1949.

"*This is a skinned and jointed rabbit mixed with two sliced onions and seasoning, and arranged in a circle in a baking tin. In the centre is a savoury heap made of ¼ lb breadcrumbs mixed with 3 oz shredded suet, pepper and salt, parsley, thyme and grated nutmeg, all bound together with an egg beaten with a little milk and sugar. Covered with rashers of bacon and baked till tender (approx. 1¾ hours at 350°—gas 4), this is delicious. Today I use a lidded baking tin instead of the ample cover of bacon and for the sugar I substitute red currant jelly or syrup*".

I find half the quantities of the "savoury heap" more than enough. It is important that the rabbit should not get dry—perhaps the best solution is to cover it with bacon and a lid as well.

One of the best rabbit dishes is the *cold Rabbit Pie* described in Chapter One.

20

Broths and soups were cheaply made with vegetables out of the garden, good dripping, and bones from the butcher. They were often thickened with bread in the old-fashioned way or given body (for these soups were often a meal) by rice, tapioca, or pearl barley.

14. Potato Soup

2 lbs potatoes	½ pint milk
1 medium-sized onion	3 tablespoons tapioca*
3 pints good stock	1 oz bacon fat
(chicken is best)	

Peel and slice potatoes and onion. Melt the fat in a large pan, and cook the vegetables in it for about 10 minutes with the lid on. Add the stock and boil for ½ hour. Rub through a sieve. Return to the saucepan, add the milk, tapioca and seasoning (plenty of salt), and simmer for another ½ hour.

*Personally I do not like tapioca so I make this soup without it. But it has been pointed out to me that what is probably meant is a kind of tapioca as fine as flour, which sets as a binding agent—arrowroot does the same job.

The flavour of the potatoes is very good; of course if they are freshly dug out of the garden it is even better. If you think of potatoes as boring I think you'll be surprised.

15. Butter Bean Soup

1 lb dried butter beans	1 pint milk
2 leeks or onions	2 quarts water
1 small carrot	seasoning
a bunch of mixed herbs	a bunch of parsley

"Cost fourpence halfpenny", it said in the margin of the recipe book; as it is filling and wholesome this seems good value and even now it doesn't cost much.

Soak the beans all night in cold water. Put them on to boil for an hour in 2 quarts of fresh water with a little salt. Chop the vegetables finely. Add them and the herbs and seasoning to the beans and simmer for another hour. Add the milk. Rub through a sieve.

16. Friar Tuck

"Take a pint of clear soup, 1 whole egg. Put on the fire to boil the soup. Beat the egg in a basin, as soup boils strain the egg through into the soup and keep on boiling till it sets".

A comforting dish, rather like chinese soup. Success depends on how good your clear soup is; chicken stock does very well.

17. Veal and Ham Pie

"Take 2 lbs of veal cutlets, ½ lb boiled ham, 2 dozen oysters, ½ lb fresh made sausages, 2 tablespoons of savoury mixed herbs, ¼ teaspoon of grated nutmeg, a little mace, pepper and salt to taste, with a strip of lemon peel finely chopped, 2 hard-boiled eggs, ½ pint of water.

"Cut the veal into square pieces. Put a layer of them at the bottom of a pie dish. Sprinkle over them a little of the herbs, spices, seasoning, lemon peel and eggs in slices and about 5 oysters and part of the sausages cut in three. Then a layer of ham in thin slices and continue till the dish is full, so as to have the ham at the top. Put puff pastry on the edge of the dish, then pour in ½ pint of water. Cover with crust and ornament with leaves, brush over with yolks of egg. Bake 1-1½ hours. When done pour in some good gravy. Mushrooms may be added to this pie".

Needless, I think, to say, you can leave out the oysters and it still makes an excellent cold pie. I add a few fillets of anchovies to the layers instead. If you cannot get good ham it is better to use bacon.

Pickling and Preserving

The making of pickles and chutneys is still so prevalent and so well covered by WI publications that I will only mention one or two that seem interesting to me.

From Miss Averil Smith's collection:

18. Rhubarb Chutney

3 *lbs Rhubarb*	1 *oz curry powder*
1 *lb sultanas*	½ *oz cayenne*
3 *onions*	1 *oz white pepper*
1 *lb brown sugar*	1 *pint malt vinegar*

Cut rhubarb in small pieces, remove the skins, mince the onions and sultanas. Place all the ingredients in a pan and heat gently for an hour, keeping them well stirred.

This was Dorothy Sitwell's recipe. She was said to be: "Very fat, and a famous horsewoman, very greedy, and had marvellous food".

19. Vegetable Marrow Pickle—Mrs. Curtis

Take a fine marrow. Peel and cut in thin slices. Sprinkle it with salt. Let it stand 24 hours. Then drain it well. 1 quart of vinegar, ¼ lb of loaf sugar, ½ oz of curry powder, a few chillies, a little cayenne pepper, 5 or 6 shallots or onions will do. Simmer from 10-15 minutes then put in your marrow and boil from 5-10 minutes and when cold it is ready for use.

Cauliflowers can be done the same way.

20. Marrow Cream

3 *lbs of marrow, 3 lbs of sugar, 6 lemons, juice and rind, 6 oz margarine.*

Boil ½ hour or more.

21. Preserving Eggs

Of course, a great deal of preserving went on in most households. Here is Mrs. Stanyon's recipe to keep eggs fresh:

3 *lbs of white quick lime*	1 *oz of cream of tartar*
10 *oz of salt*	1½ *gallons of boiling water*

Mix, stirring all the time and cover closely. When cold pour the water gently into another jar leaving the lime at the bottom of the first jar, then put in the eggs.

These eggs could then be used as fresh ones, in cooking, etc.

22. Preserving Butter I

From Miss Averil Smith of Langham's large collection of old recipes mainly gathered by her aunt, Mrs. Walsh, from many local friends, I have extracted two recipes for preserving butter and one "To double the bulk of butter" which, with today's prices might come in useful.

Brine for preserving butter:

"4 *lbs salt to 1 gallon of water. Boil the water and pour it onto the salt. Let it get quite cold. Put the butter in and cover it with 1 or more clean plates according to the amount and put a weight on (a clean stone). Then tie it all down with brown paper.*

Put more butter in with a clean fork or take out same way, never with hands. Keep it in a cool larder or cellar. You must change the brine every now and then, about 10 days or a fortnight. When changing the brine keep the butter in some plain sterilised water, cold unless you have another crock ready for it. The butter when taken out must be used soon. So best to put it in, in small quantities, say ½ lb.

23. Preserving Butter II

To Preserve Butter:

Take two parts of the best common salt, one part sugar and one part saltpetre. Beat them up together and blend the whole completely. Take 1 oz of this composition for every 16 oz of butter. Work it well into the mass and close it up for use. Butter thus cured requires to stand a month before it is begun to be used. It will then be delicious.

24. Doubling the bulk of Butter

To double the bulk of butter: To 1 lb of butter take ½ pint of milk and a small pinch of salt. Bring the milk to the boil and add the salt. Leave the milk until tepid and then heat the butter sufficiently to work the butter and milk into a paste. Leave until cold and you will find the butter is twice its original size.

The Butter Cross in Oakham

25. Preserving Yeast

Fresh supplies of yeast for baking were not easy to come by, so it had to be preserved. This method is taken from an old book on baking in Mrs. Castle's possession:

"Whisk it until it becomes thin, then take a new large wooden dish, wash it very nicely and when quite dry, lay a layer of yeast over the inside with a soft brush: let it dry, then put another layer in the same manner, and so do until you have sufficient quantity, observing that each coat dries thoroughly before another be added. It may be put on two or three inches thick, and will keep several months".

Two Fruit Preserves

A lady in Wing gave me this one:

26. Spiced Gooseberries

Take 5 lbs gooseberries, 2½ lbs sugar. Boil down thick, add spice to taste, pinch of salt and 1 pint of vinegar. Boil up together, bottle and seal until required.

27. Apple Preserve—Mrs. Castle

8 lbs apples (fallen, cooking or others—Bramley are best), weighed after peeling and coring, ½ pint of water, 5 lbs sugar, ½ pint white vinegar, 12 cloves.

Peel and slice apples. Place in container with sugar, *vinegar and water, leave standing overnight. Next day, boil altogether adding cloves in a muslin bag. Bring to boil and simmer for 45 minutes, stirring frequently. Pot and cover.*

Good for sauces and pies.

Whilst on the subject of preserving; in an old book dedicated to the memory of those killed in World War I from Rutland, I found a section on the women's work.* (It seems that farmers were extremely loath to employ women at first.)

Apparently "Fruit bottling . . . (was) carried out on a large scale in the Autumn of 1917 by Mrs. Henry Noel at Catmos. 1,000 7 lb bottles of fruit were provided for the Army. Herb growing and collection organised by the Women's Legion developed into quite an important industry in the County. Herbs were brought in the green state by growers or by school children and others who collected them in fields and woods. They were properly dried, sorted and packed by voluntary workers and then dispatched to London to be sold to the herb brokers supplying druggists all over the world".

*Rutland and the Great War: a lasting tribute to a great and noble part compiled by G. Phillips, 1920, of Padfield & Co. Ltd., Salford, Manchester.

Chapter 4

Cheeses

All the dairy farms in this area made good cheeses. In Rutland the village best known for its cheese was Braunston and the family in that village thought to make the best cheese were the Addisons. Unfortunately, although Addisons still farm there they no longer make cheese for sale.

The two cheeses most commonly made were *Stilton* and *Slipcoat* (also spelt Slip-coat or Slipcote). There is some confusion over the name Slipcoat. It means two things:
1. a soft cheese the recipe for which I will give later, and
2. a cheese which comes about by mistake in the making of Stilton.

Without wishing to enter into dispute over the origins of Stilton (numerous villages have been put forward as the place where it all started, including one in Derbyshire and, indeed, Braunston in Rutland) I think it will be agreed that the story of how it got its name is as follows:

A dairymaid employed at Quenby Hall in Leicestershire in the early eighteenth century left to marry. She took with her the recipe for a cheese already quite well-known (as Lady Beaumont Cheese, later as Quenby Cheese) and continued to make it in her own dairy at Little Dalby. One of her daughters married the landlord of the Bell Inn at Stilton in Huntingdonshire, the other a farmer in Wymondham. The latter continued to make the Quenby cheese and sent one as a present to her sister. This was so much appreciated by the customers of the Bell (which was a stage on the old Great North Road—the new A1 now by-passes Stilton) that the landlord asked his sister-in-law to supply him regularly; it became known as Stilton cheese from then on and its fame spread far and wide as the Bell's customers continued on their journeys. As far as I know it has never been made in Stilton.

There are farms and dairies in the Vale of Belvoir still making Stilton for sale (and export) but none in Rutland*.

J. Oliver writing in 1894 in a book called *Milk, Cheese and Butter* complains "So persistent have been the efforts to keep it as a monopoly of the original district in Northern Leicestershire and West Rutlandshire (sic) that it has always been difficult to obtain information concerning it". The information evidently was eventually disseminated for now Stilton can be made anywhere.

* For instance, the Long Clawson Dairy Company near Melton Mowbray, Leicestershire, who make an average of 100,000 Stiltons for sale annually. They may be ordered by post and take about four days to arrive.

Mr. Oliver did discover, however, one of the hazards of Stilton manufacture. "The coating has generally been done either in the draining room or in the making room. There is a risk in the former case of 'Slip-coat', which arises out of the lodgment within the skin of moisture which ought to come out, and which, under the influence of the warmth, produces rapid softening of the casein with sliminess".

The problem must have occurred on quite a large scale as the Ministry of Agriculture, Food and Fisheries (as it then was) in *Bulletin No. 43 on Cheesemaking* goes to the trouble of describing how to rectify the matter. "The cheese may be dusted with a mixture of flour and lime to help in the formation of another coat, but" they add disparagingly, "such cheeses will be of inferior quality".

Other people thought differently. Quoted in Florence White's *Good Things in England* is an anonymous letter dated March 15th, 1931, from someone in Leicester:

"The writer has read with much interest the notice of this cheese (Stilton) by Miss White, which appeared in today's issue of the Observer. Born in the county of Leicester 80 years since, he has 'eaten' Stilton more or less all his life. He well knows the names mentioned by Miss White—Quenby Hall and Village, Little Dalby, Wymond House, all in the centre of the famous "Quorn" country* and has known many farms which in years gone by made glorious Stilton, and has seen the great open Market Place of the County City of Leicester at the annual Cheese Fair in September in years gone by, and now never to return, filled with 'stacks' of Stilton and the famous yellow Leicestershire cheese with their makers prepared to sell them.

"I am wondering if Miss White in the course of her researches has heard of the Stilton known as 'Slipcoat'? This was so called for the reason that in some cases, the Stilton after being made and set in the cheese room to mature, for some reason, begins to 'effervesce' as it were, and, 'slipping its coat' overflows in a mass, whilst still white, creamy and immature.

"It was not exposed for sale in that form, but to some palates it was more delicious than when mature, and many times in the past, has the writer been indebted to farmer friends for a generous gift of 'Slipcoat', a pleasant memory even now, though so trivial".

To cloud the issue somewhat, I was once told by a member of the Addison family that Slipcoats (she did not mean the sort referred to above) sometimes turned into Stiltons, although she was unable to say how or why. It might be partly explained by the practice at dairies

---

* Little Dalby is of course in the Cottesmore country.

Farm Wagon starting for Leicester Fair from: Cheddar Gorge
A Book of English Cheeses by John Squire 1937

making both Stilton and Slipcoat on a large scale, of preparing one lot of curd for both cheeses. One further confusion: *In Cheeses of the World*, a USA Department of Agriculture publication, it says: "Its (the Slipcoat's) peculiarity is that when it is ready to eat (ripe), the surface softens and loosens and has a tendency to slip off". I am sure, however, that this is inaccurate and that they have been muddled, as well they might be, by the uses of the same name for two different cheeses.

The real Slipcoat, called *Colwick* in Nottinghamshire after the village there, is similar to a Cambridge although it differs slightly in the making.

A lady in Langham, Mrs. Denney, makes it like this, and I think this is how most local people would if making it at home:

28. Slipcoat

"One teaspoon of rennet to every pint of milk used. Turn the milk with rennet. Pour into muslin and hang until well drained. Cut two pieces of muslin to size of plates to be used. Place one piece of muslin on a plate, turn curd on to muslin, spread evenly. Place other piece of muslin and plate over curd. Turn plates over DAILY, once only, until required for use, i.e., four days, one week, etc., depending on how ripe cheese is required to be".

Thus, as someone described them to me: "they were as big as a dinner plate, about an inch thick; they cost sixpence and were displayed for sale on big rhubarb leaves".

In a very early recipe for Slipcoat (taken from *Agnes Bradill's Cook Book*, 1728, a ms in the Andre Simon collection) directions are given to "lead" the curd "into a clean cloth laid upon the cheese fat, the next day cover it with dock leaves and fresh nettles, so do every day, observe when the curd is come to break it with a dish and not touch it with the hand".

Anne Wilson, in *Food and Drink in Britain* talks about fresh curd cheese in the late medieval period being drained on a mat of nettle leaves and stalks; it became known as *nettle cheese*.

I have also heard locally of Slipcoats being ripened between cabbage leaves. Mrs. Waller of Lyndon told me her grandmother would wrap her cream cheeses in muslin squares and then bury them in a hole in the garden lined with rhubarb leaves to mature. These cream cheeses were made by most farmers' wives from the very creamy unpasteurised milk at their disposal.

Chapter 5

Cakes and Biscuits

Farm workers ate a great deal of cake, not dainty cream sponges but substantial, hunger-appeasing "lunch cakes" which they took with them to eat at midday. Now men can drive home for their midday meal (or to the pub maybe for what is whimsically known as a "Ploughman's Lunch"), but walking took too long, especially if you were working on a remote part of the farm.

29.   Lunch Cake

Take $\frac{1}{4}$ lb of clarified dripping, $\frac{1}{4}$ lb of ground rice, $\frac{1}{4}$ lb of currants, $\frac{1}{2}$ lb flour, one egg, 2 oz sugar, 1 teaspoonful of baking powder and enough milk to moisten it. Bake in rather a brisk oven.

30.   Plum Tussle

Mrs. Bass told me about *Plum Tussle:*

"This is the recipe both my Grannies made and what the farm workers had to eat at work. *Soak stale bread how much you want to use. Then strain and then beat up well with a fork, use any kind of Dried Fruit and Suet and Sugar (Brown) equal quantities, 1 egg optional. Beat well together. Ground spice or nutmeg can be added if prepared. Bake in a square Dripping Tin".*

Another family talked about this saying that when they felt rich they spread butter on it

In the summer when men were labouring late in the fields, the farmer's wife would send up a "field tea". These were designed for hungry men and consisted of sandwiches, a substantial cake like the *Lardie Cake* or *Spice Barm Cake* in the Feast Day chapter, and a can of tea. (In hot weather a wooden cask of home-made beer would often be attached to the harness of a cart-horse on its way up to the fields. The large coppers in most farmhouse sculleries were regularly used for home brewing till quite recently.)

Another cake for working people is *Cake in the Pan*, though this was more often eaten hot from the fire. Variations of this old recipe are made all over the country. I heard this one from an old lady in Riddlington.

31.   Cake in the Pan

1 lb flour	2 teaspoons baking powder
$\frac{1}{4}$ lb lard	$\frac{1}{2}$ lb currants
1 egg	a little milk

Mix baking powder with flour. Rub in lard and add currants. Add milk and the egg. Roll out in rounds $\frac{1}{2}$ inch thick. Cook in a greased pan (a griddle or similar flat heavy pan) turning them after about 5 minutes.

If no fruit was put in they were called *Noddn'ty* or

Noddney Cakes. (A "Nodden" cake is made at haymaking in Yorkshire and also a "Sad" cake which is very like it.) These were split and spread with jam and eaten instead of pudding on Saturdays, my informant remembered.

Family recipe books abound with sponge cakes, fruit cakes, "quick" cakes, Sally Luns, "Rich cakes for birthdays", "delicious hot cakes", "tea bread-excellent", and so on; some remembered an aunt, perhaps, famous for such-and-such cake always brought as a present on visits, someone else recalled round, flat, buttermilk cakes waiting on the fender when she came back from school. But these are family specialities, not regional and many of them appear in cookery books still. I will give only recipes that have some local connection.

32. Brooke Priory Caraway Biscuits

"These biscuits" says an article in the *Leicestershire and Rutland* magazine (September issue 1949) "will interest those who have followed the narrow turn in Oakham, over Brooke Hill and down to the lovely Priory, for it was in the old walled garden here that the maker of these biscuits grew a bush or two of caraway, and the seeds were gathered and stored in late summer for use in cakes and biscuits".

4 oz sugar, 8 oz fresh butter, 16 oz flour, 1 oz caraway seeds, and 1 egg.

Cream the butter and sugar. Add the egg yolk and beat again. Add the seeds, then the flour gradually. It will make a soft, crumbly dough. Roll out to ¼ inch thick and cut into circles, then cut each again so that you have an oval and a half-moon shape. Beat the white of egg, brush over tops of biscuits and dust with sugar. Bake on a heavy, greased tray in a moderate to slow oven (310°—gas 2) for about 15 minutes.

These quantities make about 80 small ovals and half-moons. The biscuits are very pretty and excellent, very sugary and crisp.

33. Burley Hall Queen Cakes

¼ lb butter, ¼ lb castor sugar, 6 oz self-raising flour, 3 eggs, the grated rind of a medium lemon.

Cream the butter, then add the sugar and continue till white and creamy. Add each egg with a little of the flour and mix gently. Add rind. Spoon into a greased bun tin. Bake for 10 minutes on the top shelf of a preheated oven (410°-440°, gas 7).

34. Grantham Gingerbreads

1 lb flour, 1½ lbs castor sugar, ½ lb butter, 1 oz ground ginger, 1 teaspoon bicarbonate of soda, 1 egg.

Rub the butter into the flour carefully. Add castor sugar, bicarb., and ginger and mix gently with your hands until all is equally divided and the mixture is a light brown-yellow colour.

Beat the egg in a basin. Pour it into the mixture and, again with your hands, incorporate it. Rub gently for nearly 10 minutes as the dry mixture becomes crumbly then, taking up the moisture, pastelike. You can then form a large ball of paste. Break off small pieces the size of a walnut and form into a ball, rolling it between the hands as children do with plasticine: the paste smells faintly gingery and is a deep golden colour by now. Put the balls on a greased baking sheet, flattening them slightly as you do. They will need about 15 minutes in an oven preheated to 320°, gas 3. The lady who gave me the recipe added: "Be careful in the baking as the gingerbreads should be hollow (they sometimes flop)". A timely warning, but don't let it intimidate you.

35. Belvoir Castle Buns

Belvoir Castle is the seat of the Duke of Rutland, although it is in Leicestershire. This recipe comes from the Rutland (sic) section of *Mr. Therm goes County* issued by the Gas Council in Festival Year 1951. According to the Council these buns were His Grace's favourite in 1869.

1 lb flour, 4 oz sugar, 3 oz margarine (I can't help feeling that at the Castle they might have used butter),

½ oz chopped dried fruit, ½ pint milk and water warmed, 3 oz yeast.

Rub the fat into the flour and add sugar. Cream the yeast with a little sugar and add the warm milk and water. Pour the liquid into the centre of the flour, sprinkle the dry mixture over the top, cover with a cloth and leave in a warm place until bubbles appear on the surface. (This can take 30 minutes or so, depending on temperature). At this stage mix well and knead until the dough is smooth.

You may need to add more flour. Put to rise in a warm atmosphere until its size is doubled. Knead again and roll out thinly. Sprinkle the fruit over the top and roll up like a Swiss Roll. Cut into pieces one inch wide. Place on a greased tin and allow to rise for ½ hour. Brush with a little milk. Bake for 10 minutes in a hot oven.

This amount makes a dozen large buns.

36. Bosworth Jumbles

Legend, that conveniently vague source, has it that this recipe was picked up on the battlefield at Bosworth in 1485, having supposedly been dropped by Richard the Third's cook.

½ lb sugar, ½ lb flour, 6 oz butter, 1 large egg.

Rub all together and mix the large egg. Cut into pieces the size of a walnut and make into the shape of an S

(*some say the shape of an* 8) *and "bake on a slide having been made hot"*—most people would now, I think, bake them on a tray in a medium oven till pale brown.

I think these must be the same thing as *Jumbals*, derived, according to Anne C. Wilson in *Food and Drink in Britain*, from "gemmel" or twin finger-ring. They were "fashioned as interlaced rings, knots and other such devices. Their texture varied, the paste for them sometimes resembling biscuit bread and at other times short cakes".

Chapter 6

The Pig Killing

For hundreds of years pork in all its forms has been a basic and important part of country people's diet. The poorest of people could survive if they had a pig. It is the cheapest of animals to feed: it can exist on scraps and will forage on poor land. For some farm-workers the right to graze a pig on their employer's land went with the job; though lower grade labourers who really needed this privilege were often denied it, which seems the height of meanness on the part of the landowners.

Women used to go gleaning, which was traditionally free, to feed the pigs (in extreme cases of poverty, to feed their families). Mrs. Lawrence of Preston told me how the women would then bring the gleanings to the farm to be threshed. The farmer would put aside a whole day to do this, the women each bringing a lump of coal "to keep up the steam" and a gallon of beer. The corn was taken to the local mill and ground into flour.

At Whissendine church they ran a Gleaners' Bell— you might not start until the bell had rung and must stop when the evening bell sounded. (This village also sounded a Pancake Bell during the morning of Shrove Tuesday to remind cooks.)

The right to glean goes back to early times. *Frumenty* (the name comes from the Latin for corn) must be one of England's oldest dishes; it was made from gleanings by poor people and, according to Florence White in *Good Things in England*, was offered as "a grateful and warming cup by cottagers to weary huntsmen during the season", as well as sustaining the cottagers themselves.

A pig in those days could easily weigh twenty stone by the time it was killed. One animal could feed a family for many months and the hams hanging in the cottages were "a sight better than a picture" I have often been told. Miss Ellingworth remembers her grandfather putting comfits on the bacon hanging from the ceiling— he would then shake the flitches and joints so the sweets showered down on the children.

But the editors of a WI booklet published in 1939* say that "The old-established practice of supplying the country household with bacon, fed, killed and cured on the farm, has very seriously declined since the (first) war, chiefly owing to changed economic conditions. This is much to be regretted, as the flavour of good home fed and cured bacon is excellent, and very superior to much of that purchased in shops. A supply of bacon was a great asset to the housekeeper when fresh meat was not

* *From the Farm and Garden to the Kitchen and Store Cupboard*, eds. M. Leach, U. A. Ridgway and E. A. Webb.

easy to get and shops some long distance away".

When someone was going to kill a pig, word soon got round.

It was, I quote from the same booklet, "a festival day for everyone concerned but the victim, the youngest member of the family usually claiming the "privilege" of stirring the blood to be used later on for black puddings.

"November to February inclusive are the best months for killing, owing to the colder conditions normally present at that time. After the carcase has been dressed and cut up, the flitches and hams are ready for curing. The curing room must be clean and cool, not more than 50°F.

"Dry salting can be carried out with little apparatus. The quantity of preservative for every 20 lb of meat should be 1½-2 lbs fine, dry pure salt; a little less than one ounce pure saltpetre and a little more than ½oz Demerara sugar. Saltpetre preserves the red colour of the lean meat, but, when used too liberally, hardens it. Sugar prevents hardening and shrinking. Salt preserves the meat.

"Both sides of the flitches should be rubbed with a little salt. On the following day, blood and moisture should be cleared away, and the meat, particularly the hams and shoulders, rubbed with saltpetre, followed by a rubbing with a mixture of salt and sugar. A day later salt and sugar should again be rubbed in, and the flitches turned, sprinkled with salt and left for about ten days, when they should be again turned and the lower flitch placed on top.

"At the end of three weeks or, with hams, four weeks, the bacon should be wiped with a clean cloth and hung in a warm room to dry. To prevent flies from laying eggs in the crevices, these should be freely sprinkled with pepper.

"The bacon should be placed in cotton bags, stored in a cool, airy room, and frequently examined".

Mrs. Gale of North Luffenham talked about her grandmother laying out plates for the neighbours who had kept the pig fed with scraps during the year. I have been told that Lincolnshire pigkeepers took "Pig Cheer" to their friends in a similar way. She made them look "quite artistic", arranging some kidney, liver, flead, scratchings. (Dorothy Hartley in *Food in England* says: "when no more lard could be squeezed from the scraps in the iron pot, they were 'fried to a finish' and the crisp brown pieces called 'scratchings' ").

Curiously, Mrs. Gale said, and it was corroborated by several other people, that you must never return these plates washed as this was very bad luck. I believe a similar strange superstition concerns "beastings", the first rich milk given by a cow after calving. It is illegal to sell this, but if a farmer's wife gave an old customer a jugful under no circumstances would they return the jug washed as this would bring about the death of the calf.

Yet another superstition, this one I think peculiar to this area, I found in an old edition of the *Leicestershire and Rutland Magazine*, thus: A farmer's wife in Rutland received a sitting of duck's eggs from a neighbour at nine o'clock. "I cannot imagine how she could have been so foolish", said the good woman, much distressed; and her visitor upon enquiring was told that duck's eggs brought into a house after sunset would never be hatched.

This extract, from a 1920's back number of the same magazine, describes the activities following the killing of a pig. It is from the best essay on "A Country Woman's Day" in the first round of a national WI competition and is by E. M. Cross of Frisby on the Wreake across the border in Leicestershire, but is, I think, typical of this whole area:

". . . Jimmy's sides and hams were now in the salting trough in the cellar; his head, trotters and hocks were on big dishes to be made into brawn, etc. The bones had been stewed to provide gravy, and today we are going to make pork pies.

"I get up and go downstairs, and light the big kitchen range. Soon the kettle is boiling and we have a cup of tea. The dining room is quickly swept and dusted and we have breakfast (liver and toast, and cups of tea). Beds are made, breakfast things washed, more coal fetched in, the range is stoked up, and we start the big business of the day. Mrs. Brandeth, long experienced at the job, makes the pie crust. The lard is carefully weighed, put into the big copper preserving pan with the right quantity of milk and water, and boiled. Well, the meat for the pies was cut yesterday and is in a big earthenware bowl. It is weighed, the right amount of salt and pepper added and a little of it is put into the oven in a pattypan to be tasted. The boiling lard mixture is poured into the great bowl of flour and Mrs. Brandeth mixes and kneads it in front of the fire. The wooden pie-moulds are ranged on the dresser and we start to 'raise' the pies".

I should perhaps explain here that a pork pie is usually "raised" by hand, using a mould to shape it. The moulds are of solid wood, cylindrical and often with a rounded knob on top by which to grasp it. The paste, while it is kept warm, is very pliable and you mould it round the wood quickly. As it cools it becomes hard and the moulds can be lifted out. This system is unlike that of other raised pies, game pies for example, which are baked in their decorative moulds of tin or copper (similar to those used in France for paté en croute).

"At last all the moulds are covered with warm, rich-smelling, elastic-feeling piecrust. We take them off carefully and commence to fill them with the prepared meat. A lid of pastry is put on each, it is trimmed round the edges and placed on the pastry-board ready to go to the baker's to be baked".

Incidentally, bakers also made their own pork pies and sausages for sale; it was not considered part of a butcher's business.

"There is still a little pastry left, and we want to make some sausages. The remaining meat is put through the mincing machine again; the rest of the pastry is made into sausage rolls, and several 'links' of sausage made. 'I think we will have dinner next and wash up everything afterwards; we have done a good morning's work' says Mrs. Brandeth. We have pig's fry and dry toast and a cup of tea, eaten picnic fashion by the fire".

Noted cooks would "go out pork pie making" round the villages, and a very nice job it must have been. The making of a hot water crust, for so it is called, is a most satisfying thing; akin to bread dough, it is marvellous stuff to handle and it smells so promisingly good, too. In one old notebook kept by a renowned pork pie maker from Wing, the quantities given were:

Crust: 1 stone of best flour; 5 lbs lard; 3 pints water; 3 teaspoonfuls salt.

Meat: 16 lbs pork; 4 ozs salt; 2 ozs pepper; $\frac{1}{2}$ pint water.

For those who feel inspired to try their hand at a hot water crust, here are the instructions. Bearing in mind that most people will not have a pig to kill, I give amounts which will make only two small pies. A one pound jam jar can be used instead of a mould, although it must be said that a mould produces a much nicer, rounded shape.

37. Pork Pie

12 ounces flour with a pinch of salt, 6 ounces pure pork lard, just under $\frac{1}{4}$ pint of water.

Bring the lard and water to the boil, pour on to flour. Knead (it will, obviously, be very hot indeed), till pliable and elastic. If you think the paste is too wet to mould add more flour. Having kneaded the paste to the right consistency, which does not take long, it is important to keep it at the right temperature while you start moulding. You must not let it get cold or it will become brittle. You may need to grease the bottom of the jar; in general the high proportion of lard in the paste renders this unnecessary. Take a piece of the paste and shape it round the mould as evenly as possible. The rest leave in a warm bowl, covered, on a boiler or similar warm place, or over a pan of warm water. Lift the moulds out carefully when the paste has cooled and become stiff—how long this will take depends on how wet your paste was and the temperature of your kitchen. As it dries it changes colour from the rich browny-yellow to a paler straw colour.

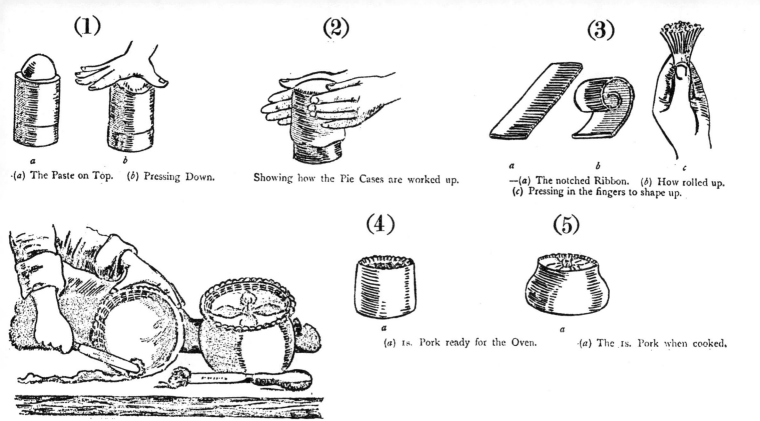

(1)

a — (a) The Paste on Top.   b — (b) Pressing Down.

(2)

Showing how the Pie Cases are worked up.

(3)

a —(a) The notched Ribbon.   b — (b) How rolled up.
c — (c) Pressing in the fingers to shape up.

(4)

a — (a) 1s. Pork ready for the Oven.

(5)

a — (a) The 1s. Pork when cooked.

Pork Pie Manufacture

From Savoury Pastry by Fredrick.T.Vine
Published Baker and Confectioner   1900

Remember to leave enough paste for the lids. These you roll out after you have filled the cases with meat. Cut a small round hole in the middle through which, later, you may pour stock. Wet the edges of both the cases and the lids, pinch together firmly and trim.

For the filling have ready two pounds of coarsely-chopped lean pork mixed with plenty of salt, pepper, sage or marjoram, and three tablespoons of water. If you tell your butcher it is for pork pies he will know what you want in the same way that he would know what you meant by steak and kidney pie meat.

The pies should stand in a cool place before baking. Bake them on a heavy sheet for $1\frac{1}{2}$ hours at about 350° (gas 3-4). When they have cooled, fill them up with the stock you have prepared in the meantime from pork bones, a trotter split in two, an onion and a good bunch of herbs. Strain and degrease it, and when it too has cooled, pour it through the holes (using a funnel) and leave to set to a jelly. Be sure to fill them right up or you will have a space between the meat, which shrinks as it cools, and the crust.

On old-fashioned market stalls pork pies always "wore" a sprig of sage and the mutton pies a sprig of mint.

It is interesting to note that a Fourteenth Century recipe quoted in *Food in England* includes "nutmeg, a large mace, and lay in your coffin good store of raisins and currants and fill with sweet butter" (coffin is the pastry case), and more recently *Cassell's New Universal Cookery Book* of 1901 confided the same hint to its readers thus: "We may mention that at a certain farm-house in the Midlands, the pork pies are always made with layers of stoned raisins between the layers of pork. We never met with these pies elsewhere, but can recommend them".

Anchovy sauce is traditionally added round Melton. It makes the inside of the pie slightly pink instead of that dispiriting grey and improves the flavour—only a small amount is needed.

38. Brawn

Mrs. Castle's Recipe for Brawn:

Take pig's face and trotters or hock pieces and simmer in water till the meat drops off the bone. Strain the juice and chop the meat. Add plenty of fresh sage, salt and pepper and leave to set in bowl or mould.

Brawn is usually eaten with a mustard sauce—Oxford Brawn Sauce is justly famous—but a pot of mustard on the table is good too.

A Brawn Sauce from *Common Sense Cookery* by Col. Kenney Herbert, published in 1905 by Edward Arnold:

39. Brawn Sauce

Beat together in a basin with a fork by degrees three tablespoonfuls of salad oil, with one and half of vinegar, a good dessertspoonful of made mustard, and the same of sifted sugar: add the juice and rasped zest of an orange, and season with a saltspoonful of salt and half one of pepper.

If you are lucky you can sometimes buy brawn at the WI market in Oakham. Few people make their own *sausages* now, but just in case, here is Mrs. Curtis's recipe:

40. Sausages

4 lbs of lean pork, 3 lbs of fat (minced), 1 oz salt, ¼ oz pepper, 3 teaspoonfuls of sage, nutmeg (if liked), a slice of bread off a large loaf an inch thick; soaked in cold water. Mix well and fill the skins.

Haslets were made in all the villages when a pig was killed. They were described to me by Miss Lane of Burley as being pig's liver minced with herbs and seasoning, wrapped in a piece of the Veil from the lining of the pig's stomach, baked for a short time and eaten cold. (Other people used a mixture of heart, kidneys and liver.) This is a much richer dish than the haslets made in Hampshire and Shropshire, for example, where they use lean pork and bread or breadcrumbs. In Wales, I believe, they make a similar dish called Cawl Haslet, with liver, onion and potatoes, served hot. The version sold by Oakham butchers now seems to contain more sausage meat than liver.

Savoury Ducks and *Faggots* are all of the same family.

41. Black Puddings

Black Puddings (from From the Farm and Garden to the Kitchen and Store Cupboard).

¼ teaspoon ground nutmeg	¼ teaspoon pimento
½ teaspoon sage	1 lb pearl barley
½ gallon pig's blood	½ lb onions
4 ozs salt	1¾-2 lbs beef fat
1 lb flour	

Sieve together the dry ingredients, mix to a paste with some of the blood, add the rest, mix with fat chopped in small cubes, pearl barley and onions partly boiled and finely chopped. Fill skins and simmer in plenty of water for 20 minutes. This mixture makes about 12 lbs of puddings.

People often say "nothing was wasted of a pig, only the squeak was uneaten". Even the ears and tail could be made into a consommé. The lard rendered down was precious; it supplied the house for many months with fat for pastry and cake making.

Any scraps and bones left from pie making could be made into a *bony pie*. This was a dish that many poor families knew only too well, occurring with monotonous regularity when meat was too expensive and goodness from bones had to suffice. But in some places the left-overs of all the pig-killing by-products were made into a dish pie (i.e., not a raised pie). A piece of the hot water crust was used for a top, it was baked and eaten when all the work of pies, sausages, etc., was over. A richer version is the *Leicestershire or Medley pie*, sometimes made in a cake tin lined with hot water crust, and usually including apple as well as pork, and enriched with ale.

APPENDIX

Clipsham Plough Boys' Song
As related by Mrs. Wilson of Clipsham

(1) Characters

No. 1 Head Man   This act was performed
No. 2 Fool   by the boys from
No. 3 Thrasher Blade (Man) different farms in
No. 4 The Doctor   the village on the
No. 5 Servant Man   second Monday in
No. 6 Soldier   January, known as
No. 7 Lady   Plough Monday.
No. 8 Hopper Joe

(1st) Head man enters and Tom Fool and No 3 follows
Good people give attention and listen to my song,
I will tell you of the Plough Boys before the time
is long,
To see how we do toil and moil without a dread or fear,
And you'll see us Plough Boys labouring all seasons
of the year.

Head man turning to Tom Fool says
Hello, my good man, and what are you doing here?

Tom Fool replies
I have come to learn the arts of industry.

Head man
Arts of industry! and pray who are you?

Tom answers
Well, you have heard of all these Jack Fools and Bob
Fools,
Well, I am none of them,
I am what they call the real old Tom Fool.

Enter Thrasher Blade and says
Behold the mighty thrasher blade,
Good people all doth know,

My old Dad learnt me this trade,
Just ninety years ago.
I've thrashed around this county, and many others too.
At last I went down to the battle of Waterloo,
Thrashed old Bonaparte and all his crew,
And now, Tom, I will thrash you.

Tom
Oh no, you won't!

Thrasher
Oh yes, I shall!

Tom
Oh no, you will not—for my head is made of brass
And my body's made of steel,
And no mortal man can make me feel.

Fool
I should like to see you do't.

*The Thrasher man proceeds to hit Tom with his blade
carried for the job until the Head man slips in and tries to
stop him from hurting Tom.*

Head man and others call out
Oh see, oh see what thou has done!
Laid poor Tom beneath the evening sun
As he lies bleeding on this cold floor
Faith, (and) to rise no more.

Thrasher man says
All cry £5 for a Doctor, £10 to keep away!
Doctor comes running in

Head man
What, you a Doctor?

Doctor replies looking around
I see no peg
I'll hang my hat upon the floor.
Yes I've travelled England, Ireland, Scotland
                                    and Wales,
And come back to old England again.

Head man
What can you cure, my man?

*Doctor has wooden specs (Spectacles) and takes a pill
from large wooden box.*
I can cure ipsey-pipsey, palsey, gout,
Pains within and pains without.

Doctor then feels his pulse looking at his watch and says
His pulse beating 99 times to my watch strikes one,
Here, Tom, take this pill,
If the pill don't digest the box will.
This old man he is not dead, he's only in a trance;
So raise him up and we'll have a dance:

If he can't dance we can sing,
So raise him up and we'll begin.

(*All*) *Sing*
"There's a good time coming boys—wait a little
longer".

In comes I the servant man,
Oh don't you see my whip in hand?
As I go forth to plough the land
I turn it upside down;
As straight I go from end to end
I scarcely make one baulk or bend
And to my horses I attend
As they go gaily round the end.
Gee whoa—back there!

In comes I the recruiting Sergeant
I've had orders from the Queen
To enlist all young men that follow cart-horse or
Plough.

Servant man
Will thou list me, my good man?

Reply from Sergeant
Yes if you are willing.
In your hand I'll place this shilling,
And ten bright guineas shall be your bounty,
if along with me you'll go,

And your old hat will be trimmed with ribbons
And you will cut a gallant show.

Servant man
Yes, kind sir, I'll take your offer,
Time will quickly pass.
Dash my wig if I'll grieve any longer,
For that proud and saucy lass.

Enter Lady singing
Behold the lady bright and gay,
Good fortune and sweet charms,
Though scornful I was thrown away,
Right out of my true love's arms;
He swears if I don't wed with him,
As you may understand,
He'll list for a soldier,
And go to some foreign land.

Servant man
Does thou love me, my pretty maid?

Lady
Yes.

Servant man
And when shall be our wedding day?
We will shake hands and we'll be wed,

And we'll make banns tomorrow,
And I'll ask all you Tom Fools and Jack Fools to me
and my wife's wedding.
And I tell you what we will have for dinner.—A leg of
a Lark and Louse roasted.
So you can bolt about.
And get your knives sharpened for there will not be
much gravy flying about.

No. 8 Hopper Joe
In comes I old Hopper Joe,
I can either plough, sow reap or mow,
I hope the master will bestow,
All he can afford us all.

*He collects and they sing: "There's a good time coming
boys wait a little longer" and other songs.*
Success unto our masters and mistresses too.
Likewise the little children that round the table go.

Good master and good mistress you see our fool has
gone.
We make it our business to follow him along.
We thank you for your civility and what you gave us
here.
We wish you all Good Night and another Happy Year.

Tom Fool says
I can't see much in that old Hopper yet.

Headman
What do you want to see in that old Hopper, Tom?
Bone pies, mince pies, and pork pies, etc.?

———————

For to plough and to sow
and to reap and to mow
and to be a farmer's boy
and to be a farmer's boy